Songs
of the
Stones
Oracle

Cards to connect you
to the Earth and her
guardians

W0019005

Katie-Jane Wright

Illustrated by Nikki Strange

Song of the Stones Oracle
Katie-Jane Wright
Illustrated by Nikki Strange

First published in the UK and USA in 2025 by
Watkins, an imprint of Watkins Media Limited
Unit 11, Shepperton House, 83–93 Shepperton Road
London N1 3DF

enquiries@watkinspublishing.com

Design and typography copyright © Watkins Media Limited 2025
Text copyright © Katie-Jane Wright 2025
Artwork copyright © Nikki Strange 2025

The right of Katie-Jane Wright to be identified as the Author of
this text has been asserted in accordance with the Copyright,
Designs and Patents Act of 1988.

All rights reserved. No part of this book may be reproduced in
any form or by any electronic or mechanical means, including
information storage and retrieval systems, without permission
in writing from the publisher, except by a reviewer who may
quote brief passages in a review.

Commissioning Editor: Ella Chappell
Managing Editor: Sophie Blackman
Project Editor: Brittany Willis
Head of Design: Karen Smith
Designer: Sneha Alexander
Production: Uzma Taj

A CIP record for this book is available from the British Library

ISBN: 978-1-78678-870-2

10 9 8 7 6 5 4 3 2 1

Printed in China

www.watkinspublishing.com

The manufacturer's authorised representative in the EU for product
safety is eucomply OÜ - Pärnu mnt 139b-14, 11317 Tallinn, Estonia,
hello@eucompliancepartner.com, www.eucompliancepartner.com

Contents

Note from the Author

I have always experienced the stones of the Earth talking to me, along with the crystal devas and the guardian energies that surround them. To hold a stone and to hear the whispers of the Earth is something that is symbiotic to me, because all of nature is part of us. I created this deck to help you to connect with the wisdom that the stones provide for us.

I come from an ancestral line of the Khasi clan of northeast India. The Khasi believe that nature is our library. They worked closely with stones and plants, and many ancient megaliths stand in their sacred hills, and I feel the healing power and medicine of these stones within my heart and my hands.

My ancestors have a saying:

Mei- Ri- Sawkun

This is an indigenous Khasi concept, meaning:

Mother Earth cradles its children and all else around it.

There is an ancient healing song that rises up through Mother Earth's roots, a song of hope and unity, of compassion and love: the ancient ones are asking us to be still and listen. Through this deck, we can find this stillness and the space to connect with the voices of the Earth and its heartbeat and sounds, like the Khasi people do. Mother Earth cradles us through the "Songs of the Stones", creating a space for nature to sing, and for the stones, the plants and animals to pass on their wisdom. The Earth has a great many gifts for us; let us receive these through this deck.

I thank you for the opportunity to create this deck. Writing it has been a beautiful process, spanning years of travel where I have connected to the Songs of the Stones, and Earth's grids and stones in so many places, from the flint of Avebury, to the obsidian of Mexico and the red rock of Sedona's vortexes to the sea coal washed up on the beaches of the Northumbrian coast. I hope that you feel the love and energy woven through this deck and enjoy working with it as much as I have enjoyed writing it.

Katie-Jane

Mother Earth, how can I best serve you?

The Earth replied —

Why do you feel I need your service?
All I need is balance.
*Just **be** here with me.*

I am complete, I flow, expand, release and regulate.
I am whole.
Are you not the same?
Breathe with me as the tide does.

We are perfection.
Creation is in the eye of the mind and the heart
of the whole.

Do not busy yourself with what you think you should
be doing, let it flow.

Be one with the Earth and sky
Be at one with perfection.

*Just **be**,*
It is all so simple to me.

Introduction

Light Language

Sometimes words can be so limiting, and the heart speaks in colours and tones the brain cannot comprehend. As such, you'll notice golden energetic coding sprinkled though the illustrations in this deck. These symbols are the coded language of light. They are not for the mind, but for the heart.

Look out for these symbols as you use the deck. They are sometimes formed by lines, dashes and dots, and sometimes in more geometric shapes, or are more fluid and flow across the cards like text. These sacred shapes layer and move, and each stroke of the pen is imbued with higher frequencies that are channelled and embodied through the heart as I scribe them. Energy flows through them like a river; when you draw these cards and gaze at them, ancient parts of you awaken. They are multi-dimensional living things that exist on other planes; when I bring them through my heart I sing tones and frequencies that impress through them. Created with intent, they are not for the mind to process but for the heart to feel. They are sacred geometry, which is what all nature represents in its own way, and they will interact with your body's energetic field by travelling through it once you accept it into your field.

The Elements

$$\triangledown \quad \triangle \quad \triangledown \quad \triangle$$

From left to right: Earth, Air, Water, Fire. It's good to keep an eye on these elemental symbols through your readings – more about this on page 15.

Chakras

Through this deck focus will be brought to key energy centres in the body. There are seven main chakras situated along the spine, from the base to the crown of your head. They govern the flow of energy through the body, regulating it, spinning clockwise or anticlockwise, and open front and back through the lightbody (the energy field around and connected to us, which includes the auric field), connecting it to all of you including the emotional, mental and physical layers of your aura.

Through the deck you may be asked to focus more healing on specific chakra centres that may be blocked or not running as fast or efficiently as usual.

I ask that you expand your awareness to the earth star chakra, which is 30–46cm/12–18in below your feet in the Earth. The higher chakras above are the crown, the soul star, the Stella gateway, the universal chakra, the galactic chakra and the divine gateway. As human consciousness expands through our evolution cycle we must be moving energies consciously through our highest galactic chakras, descending down into our crown and ascending up through our earth star chakra and into our root to ground in a full and solid way.

These are all the known colours of the chakras:

Soul star chakra: magenta pink or pure white
Stella gateway: pure gold
Crown: white
Third eye: violet
Throat: blue
Heart: green
Solar plexus: yellow
Sacral: orange
Root: red
Earth star: brown

The colours of the galactic chakras are still under debate.

The Colour Rays

It is important when working with energies and crystals that we invoke the coloured ray they represent for healing. Amethyst, for example, is a violet ray that can be called upon and brought down through the body. By invoking and working with the coloured rays we bring more focused intent to our healing, Colours carry unique vibrational frequencies that affect the body's energy systems. For example, green is the colour of nature, love, balance, healing and cellular growth, so working with the emerald ray would support this.

I also recommend noticing any patterns of colours that are coming through the cards for you. If, for example, you are seeing a lot of blue in your spreads it is a message to focus on your throat chakra, which is blue. These are the ray colours:

* **The first ray is blue:** it connects with the throat and the ascended master El Morya, and represents willpower, truth and balance.
* **The second ray is yellow:** it connects with the crown and the ascended master Kuthumi, and represents wisdom, understanding and illumination.
* **The third ray is pink,** the ray of divine love: it connects with the heart and the ascended master

Paul the Venetian, and it holds the energies of love and beauty.

✳ The fourth ray is white: it connects with the root and the ascended master Serapis Bey, and it represents purity, joy and resurrection.

✳ The fifth ray is green: it connects with the third eye and master Hilarion, and it represents, science, wisdom and the healing arts.

✳ The sixth ray is purple: it connects with the solar plexus and Lady Master Nada, and it represents service and peace.

✳ The seventh ray is violet: it connects with the sacral chakra and Master Saint Germain, and it represents freedom and compassion.

Maiden, Mother, Crone

These will come up throughout this booklet. The Maiden represents the first stage of the lunar cycle: the waxing moon. She is a free spirit that radiates positive energy and shapes our dreams, wishes and aspirations.

The Mother is the second stage of the lunar cycle: the full moon. She holds wisdom and balance, is full of confidence and offers empowerment through the power of reflection.

The Crone is the third stage of the lunar cycle: the

waning moon. She teaches how to accept all facets of life, bringing peace and inner calm, which gives us the ability to understand and control our emotions.

"Shamanic"

The word "shamanic" is a spiritual temple that describes a collection of ancestors from different tribes or traditions. My ancestors are shamans and medicine people, and my understanding of this term comes through them.

How to Work with the Deck

The Gateway Cards

There are eight gateway cards in this deck, and when one is attracted to you, it is a sign that high-frequency activations and alignments are coming. They are the "singers" of this deck, bringing pure tones for change.

These gateway cards hold potent energetic frequencies for you to meditate with. The Earth and stars are one: as above so below, and we see the marriage of Earth and cosmic energies through these portal cards.

For a more detailed analysis of each of the eight gateway cards, see pages 22–37.

How to Work with the Energies of the Gateways

If one of these cards picked you, you have some focused work to do around this gateway. It is time to look at increasing the flow of love through your body. Take some time to sit with this card, and perhaps light a candle and place it in your healing space so you can see it often to remind you of this gateway, and the flow of love through your body.

* Softly gaze at the energetic gateway, imagining it jumping from the page and hovering in the space between you, taking on its own consciousness, spinning, each piece moving individually and as a whole.
* Take a moment to close your eyes and breathe, call the gateway into yourself to sit in the centre of your higher heart.
* In your heart it spins faster, expanding and contracting, sending ripples of light and song through you as you receive its elevating energies.
* Allow it to move through your heart in the way it wishes, just observing and allowing, not attaching. Notice the sensations and flow, and any messages or images that come to you in this moment.

Elemental Symbols

Keep an eye on the elements that show up for you in a reading, as certain elements may appear repeatedly and this could be a sign to take notice of. Perhaps you need more of that element. For example, if the Earth symbol is appearing a lot in the cards you are drawing, it could be telling you that you need more grounding in your life.

Card Layouts

Daily Medicine (one card)
Sometimes all you need to do is pull one card and ask a question to receive clear guidance on where you are currently in your life. When I work with this layout, I like to ask:

What energies do I need to work with going forwards?

Spirit Drum Spread (five cards)
This is an empowering card spread, offering direction and focus on a situation you may be struggling with. By harnessing all of the elements in this circular card

layout, the ancestors will sing, dance and drum with you, to stimulate creative flow, solve problems and bring reason to whatever you are facing. It's a highly empowering spread for calling in clarity and focus.

Before you begin, take a moment to hold this deck to your heart and thank it for what you are about to receive. You may wish to light a candle and set it down in the centre of the card circle: this flame is a symbol of gratitude and light and represents your spirit and the memory of your ancestors.

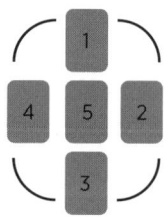

Card 1: What am I seeking?
Card 2: How do I call it in?
Card 3: How will the Earth support me?
Card 4: What do I need to let go of?
Card 5: What will strengthen as a result of this?

The Thunderbird Spread (four cards)

This is a spread to bring support and positive change into yourself.

The Thunderbird permeates the spiritual world of many Native American groups. In Native American myths, they are powerful, life-giving spirits, who command the storm clouds and create thunder and lightning with the beating of their wings. The spread will cause an electric shake-up for you, supporting you by bringing in new, positive changes.

The Thunderbird Spread is a perfect spread to do after any shadow work, at the start of new adventures, projects and opportunities, and follows on nicely from the Spirit Drum Spread.

Before you work with this spread, hold the deck to your heart and speak out loud,

I am ready for change.
I am ready for change.
I am ready for change.

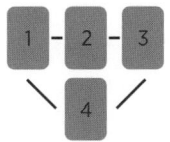

Card 1: Where do I need to anchor change in my body?
Card 2: How can I do this?
Card 3: What obstacles do I need to overcome to expand with this change?
Card 4: What is ready to fall away?

The Wishbone Spread (five cards)

This is an abundance spread, to help you harness the high frequencies of luck, joy and good fortune to create whatever you are dreaming of.

An ancient Italian civilization known as the Etruscans used chicken bones in divination, believing that birds could tell the future. The use of birds for fortune telling was widespread at that time. The bird's "wishbone" (or furcula) was dried out and saved, and the Etruscan people would hold and gently stroke it while making their wishes. This deck takes influence from the Etruscans methods.

Before you begin, hold in your heart the vision and feeling of what you are wishing for. Let that image unfold and expand, warming you as it spreads and touches all parts of you. Place the cards to your heart and say:

Divine energies, please support me in manifesting my hopes and dreams.

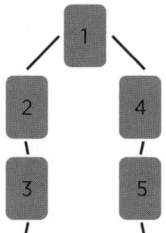

Card 1: Which energies wish to support me in manifesting my wishes?
Card 2: What do I need to focus on to support my vision?
Card 3: What should I call in to support my vision further?
Card 4: Are there any blocks I need to address to make this vision a reality?
Card 5: How can I release these blocks effectively?

Three-Month Forecast

This is a good spread for finding framework and structure. To use it, pull a card to represent each month, and ask:

What do the energies of (name of the month)
have to offer me?

Each card gives you an idea of the energies resonant for you during that month, and you can identify patterns of rest and creativity, elements to work with or chakras to focus on (by noticing colour patterns) using this spread.

It also offers you a method to feel into what is coming for you in the next few months. I tend to keep this to a three-month spread, as energies shift and change so fast, and we also have the ability to shape and change our future. But you can also do a six-month or even a 12-month overview if you want to.

Below is a very simple example of the card forecast for three months:

Card 1: January
Card 2: February
Card 3: March

THE CARDS

Divine Feminine Gateway

MEANING:

The answer is love

This gateway card shows a golden code to support the opening of the heart and sacral chakra, and the Divine Feminine Gateway brings energies to help your heart accept what is. It is a heart activation that will soften the heart, helping it unfold and open gently, like a rose. It's a divine feminine energy that connects you to Venus, the cosmic heart and the mystery school teachings of wisdom through love. The card was brought through to me in Mary Magdalene's basilica in the south of France. As I sat above her crypt, the energies flowed and a group of women sang, and this card appeared in my third eye.

How to work with the energies of this card

If this card picks you, you have some focused work to do around this gateway. It is time to look at increasing the flow of divine love through your body. Like the Pink Kunzite Higher Heart Gateway card, the Divine Feminine Gateway connects and aligns the heart's chambers, and opens them to energy and love. Take some time to sit with this card, and perhaps light a candle and place it in your healing space to remind you of this card and the flow of love through your body.

✳ Softly gaze at the energetic gateway, imagining it jumping from the page and hovering in the space between you, taking on its own consciousness, spinning, each piece moving individually and as a whole.

✳ Take a moment to close your eyes and breathe, call the gateway into your heart to seat itself in the centre.

✳ It spins there, faster, expanding and contracting, sending ripples of light and song through you, as you receive its elevating energies.

✳ Allow it to move through your heart in the way it wishes, just observing and allowing, not attaching. Notice the sensations and flow, and any messages or images that come in this moment.

Earth Star Gateway

MEANING:
Flower codex

This card shows a golden code for the earth star chakra, holding the energies of nature and flowers. The Earth flourishes below our feet. It is a vast library of flora and fauna that cannot be found anywhere else in this Solar System. This gateway code activates dormant plant wisdom within your crystalline codex. It helps you to remember your gifts and ways of working with plant medicine, speaking to the elemental aspects of you that exist in other places: the fae, elven and pixie, igniting the fire and remembrance in your earth star chakra.

How to work with the energies of this card

If this card picks you, you are going on a journey with the flowers and plants to awaken old energy pathways within you from the ground up. Consider taking time to connect with the flowers and trees. Read about and craft oils and tinctures, learn more from the flowers, pick one that has been singing to you and sit with it in your home for a week, listening, tending to it if you can. Form a relationship with it and ask it:

How do you know my ancestors?

✴ Softly gaze at the energetic gateway, imagine it jumping from the page and hovering in the space between you, taking on its own consciousness, spinning, each piece moving individually. Imagine it is blooming with flowers and there are green vines growing through it, reaching out to you.

❋ Take a moment to close your eyes and breathe, calling the gateway into your body.

❋ In your body, it spins faster, expanding and contracting, sending ripples of light and song through you as you receive its earthy energies.

Allow it to move through your body in the way it wishes, just observing and allowing, not attaching. Notice the sensations and flow, and any messages or images that come in this moment.

Herkimer Crown Gateway

MEANING:

Detach from the 3D matrix and rise above

This card shows the golden code and the Herkimer diamond. The Herkimer gateway brings in the energies of elevation, clearing and cleansing to the higher chakras. This gateway card is for a crown activation: to open the crown and receive into your physical body the highest frequencies you can hold. These will then exist in harmony through all the layers of your being.

It connects and moves energies through the third eye, soma, crown and soul star chakras. Working with the pure diamond ray of cleansing and clarity as it shines through you, the Herkimer Crown Gateway allows for a process of purification to begin and move through and down into your body. This sets in motion more "emptying", which will allow your being to expand.

How to work with the energies of this card

If this card picks you, you have some focused work to do around this gateway. It is time to look at increasing the diamond flow of purity and clarity through your body. Take some time to sit with this card, and perhaps light a candle and place it in your healing space to remind you of this card and the flow of love through your body.

* Softly gaze at the energetic gateway, imagining it jumping from the page and hovering in the space between you, taking on its own consciousness, spinning, each piece moving individually and as a whole.
* Take a moment to close your eyes and breathe, and call the gateway into your crown.
* In your crown, it spins faster, expanding and contracting, sending ripples of light and song through you as you receive its elevating energies.
* Allow it to move through your higher chakras

or body in the way it wishes, just observing and allowing, not attaching. Notice the sensations and flow, and any messages or images that come in this moment.

Lemurian Diamond Gateway

MEANING:
Fifth-dimensional frequencies

Lemuria was heaven on Earth, a place that was so crystalline it sang; the waters were pure and all of nature danced with high fifth-dimensional energy. It had a peaceful race of beings who existed millions of years ago. The Lemurian Gateway brings forth the energies of diamond and rainbow rays, high-frequency elemental rays that were flowing through our Earth at that time. This gateway takes you to the Lemuria you remember in your heart – a tropical paradise – and this card is about support and remembering the truth of who you are and how you are connected to the whole. Paint a picture around you of the lush tropical paradise on the card, peppered with deep green fern plants and bright red hibiscus flowers. In the distance you hear the sparkle of water and see a waterfall through the palms. You transport yourself to this Lemuria, where the Earth glistens with rainbow hues, every part of nature around you sings and moves in joy. This is truly the garden of paradise we often read about.

We hold this vision of Golden Lemuria together now and fifth-dimensional frequencies re-awaken through your waters. Take a few breaths of this glorious energy around you. It enters your body like treacle, nurturing and warm: it is now home.

How to work with the energies of this card

✳ Softly gaze at this Lemurian gateway, imagining it jumping from the page and hovering in the space between you, creating an ever-growing portal of diamond light that shines brightly in your space.

✳ Take a breath and call it into your heart and third eye.

✳ As it connects, feel it glow brighter with each breath.

✳ Call in the angels and beings of Lemuria to hold you in a sphere of diamond light.

✳ Ask the Pleiadian council of light that supported the seeding of the Lemurian crystals into the grid to come forward to surround you in a sphere of their light.

✳ Receive the golden light language into your aura.

✳ Observe and witness the wonder, thanking the star guides and ancestors for their potent energies of remembrance.

✳ Hold onto this code in your heart and breathe in its

golden glow, absorbing its light language as it flows into your heart, body, organs, bones, cells and waters.
✳ Take your time feeling and breathing its energy, connecting with the guides and receiving anything they wish to offer you.

Malachite Birthing Gateway

MEANING:

A time to create

This Malachite Birthing Gateway card brings the energies of change and creation to help you begin new projects, new relationships and endeavours, and shows a golden code to support the womb with the energies of Malachite. It marks a start of something creative that you are calling forward. It is a sacral activation that will stir creative energies and assist you in birthing other, brand-new energies, projects and ideas. It can also act as a fertility code to support birthing new life. The card brings through the emerald ray, the fifth ray of truth, healing and science to channel through the body.

Malachite is known as the midwife stone, because of its ability to help you move through huge transitions. It encourages us to embrace change and emotional risk-taking, and its green layers draw out impurities and stimulate life-force energy into your aura. This connects us with the deep healing energy of nature, reminding us of the beauty of this world in the flowers, roots, plants and trees.

How to work with the energies of this card
If this card picks you, you have support in birthing new frequencies and ideas. Take some time to sit with this card, and perhaps light a candle and place it in your healing space to remind you of this card and the flow of love through your body.

* Softly gaze at the energetic gateway and its glowing emerald light. Imagine it jumping from the page and hovering in the space between you, taking on its own consciousness, spinning, each piece moving individually and as a whole, as its emerald light enters your space.
* Take a moment to close your eyes and breathe, and call the gateway into your sacral chakra.
* In your sacral chakra it spins faster, expanding and contracting, sending ripples of light and song through you as you receive its emerald energies.
* Allow it to move through your body in the way it wishes, just observing and allowing, not attaching.

Notice the sensations and flow, and any messages or images that come in this moment.

Pink Kunzite Higher Heart Gateway

MEANING:

The only way is in and through

This card shows a golden code and the energies of Pink Kunzite. The Pink Kunzite brings energies to expand your heart, bringing clarity and focus to heart-based decisions. This gateway card is for a thymus activation, to elevate the link between the heart complex (which lies between the heart and the throat) with emotionally soothing frequencies. It brings calm waters through rising storms, steering energy in and up to your higher heart, working with the third ray of divine love to bring it into focus in your heart centre. Then you can face whatever is moving through your heart in a loving, compassionate and confident way. Kunzite opens the heart to the energies of love and embraces all types of love: love for yourself, the community, the animals and plants, the Earth and all it holds. This high vibrational clarifying energy brings peace and security to the heart.

How to work with the energies of this card

If this card picked you, you have some focused work to do around this gateway. It is time to look at increasing the flow of love through your body. Take some time to sit with this card, and perhaps light a candle and place it in your healing space to remind you of this card and the flow of love through your body.

✳ Softly gaze at the energetic gateway, imagining it jumping from the page and hovering in the space between you, taking on its own consciousness, spinning, each piece moving individually and as a whole.

✳ Take a moment to close your eyes and breathe, call the gateway into yourself to seat in the centre of your higher heart.

✳ In your higher heart it spins faster, expanding and contracting, sending ripples of light and song through you as you receive its elevating energies.

✳ Allow it to move through your heart in the way it wishes, just observing and allowing, not attaching. Notice the sensations and flow, and any messages or images that come in this moment.

Red Jasper Root Gateway

MEANING:

Focus on grounding

This gateway card shows a golden code for the root chakra, and the energies of this card bring stabilizing and grounding energy to the root, and they ask you to explore what this coding evokes in you. It is for a root activation, to ground you fully into your body. Perhaps you are in need of more potent grounding, fresh ways, and new crystal allies to bring you this grounding.

Red Jasper has a rich and varied history, with a link to the energy of the blood through its colour and energy, which is due to a high iron content. It was revered by many ancient peoples as a powerful stone of protection. This ranged from warriors who used it for physical protection around their energy field to Native Americans who worked with its energy during their practice of spirit walking. It was also called "the blood of Mother Earth" by Native American tribes because it was believed to detoxify and staunch the flow of blood from wounds.

Red Jasper's medicine steps forward to bring stabilizing, focused and fast grounding energies to your aura.

How to work with the energies of this card

If this card picks you, you have some focused work to do on your root, whether it's root grounding or expansion that is needed. Take some time to sit with this card and perhaps light a candle and place it in your healing space so you can see it often and remind yourself of this card.

✺ Softly gaze at the energetic gateway, imagining it jumping from the page and hovering in the space between you, taking on its own consciousness, spinning, each piece moving both individually and as a whole.

✺ Take a moment to close your eyes and breathe, calling the gateway into your root.

✺ In your root it spins faster, expanding and contracting, sending ripples of red light and song through you as you receive its nurturing and earthy energies.

Allow it to move through your lower chakras or your body in the way it wishes, just observing and allowing, not attaching to them. Notice the sensations and flow, and any messages or images that come in this moment.

Womb Gateway

MEANING:

Bee maiden awaken

This gateway card shows the golden code that connects to the energy of the bee, and brings its activational womb energies, which are also a symbol of the mysteries of the divine feminine. This card's energies support a restoration, rejuvenation and cleanse of the womb/sacral area. It will activate your cellular memory and connection to the ancient "Melissae" bee priestesses. Working with its energies will support you in moving through the deepest caverns of your womb to clear, purify, witness and heal.

How to work with the energies of this card

If this card picks you, you have support in accessing deeper womb wisdom, and the opportunity to call forward and heal ancestral trauma. Take some time to sit with this card, and perhaps light a candle and place it in your healing space to remind you of this card and the flow of love through your body.

✳ Softly gaze at the energetic gateway and its glowing golden light. Imagine it jumping from the page, and hovering in the space between you, taking on its own consciousness, spinning, each piece moving individually and as a whole. You might even hear the faint sound of bees buzzing.

✷ Take a moment to close your eyes and breathe, and call this gateway into your womb.

✷ In your womb it spins faster, expanding and contracting, sending ripples of light and song through you as you receive its golden energies.

✷ Allow it to move through your body in the way it wishes, just observing and allowing, not attaching. Notice the sensations and flow, and any messages or images that come in this moment.

Alexandrite

ELEMEMT:
Water, Fire ▽△

MEANING:
*Stillness is required
for deeper healing*

Alexandrite is the light of shifting frequencies, change, transformation and cleansing, and you can see on the card how its colours shift and range depending on the light. It brings its light into your being where fear once hid and helps you make a quantum leap to the highest and greatest frequency timelines. It is supporting you to embrace and navigate these shifts in your personal growth and development.

Alexandrite is an extremely powerful healing tool. It helps you process your feelings and find emotional maturity. If you have found its energy now, it is supporting you to begin a great shift in your inner and outer worlds. It has a detoxifying and cleansing action of toxins, chemicals and impurities, so if you have pulled this card today perhaps it's time to look at what products you are using on your body, in your home or consuming.

When Alexandrite spoke to me, it wished to focus very specifically on the message of rest and recovery, crucial elements for healing. It works very closely with the physical layer of the body/aura by offering the power to restore your body back to full health, encouraging healthy blood circulation and cleansing the internal organs.

It is time to pull you into the depths of your healing, into the waters of your being, to embrace the beautiful darkness within – the stillness and quietness of the darkness that can bring you back to your centre, to the zero point field of creation. To enter the dark caverns within you is to enter into stillness, and to be still is to receive.

All that is wished for you at this time is to be still

and receive. Alexandrite can help you heal the deepest wounds, she is ready and willing, but you must rest. Sometimes the universe forces us to rest if we do not listen, so please listen now: your physical body is tired and needs tending to.

Ammonite

ELEMEMT:
Earth, Air ▽ △

MEANING:
Aligning to your purpose; the spiral; renewal

The pearlized Ammonite on this card with its soft glow and flowing watery energy around it is asking to bring you to a place of acceptance of the past. When we learn from our ancestral past we can change and grow.

Ammonites are an extinct group of mollusc animals that date back to 420 million years ago. Because they were alive and well during a very different world than we live in today, they hold records of those ancient energies for us to learn from and connect with. They imbue you with the energies of strength, longevity and perseverance.

Ammonite holds the ancient knowledge of Earth within it. Gazing into its spirals can take you through and beyond the origins of Earth and into the structure of the universe itself for inter-dimensional exploration. It's a powerful Earth healing tool that has absorbed cosmic energy over eons of time to help stimulate the life force (Chi) within you.

Kundalini is the sexual energy stored at the base of the spine, sometimes referred to as shakti. Both men and women have it, and when you work with that energy and bring it consciously up the spine to the crown, you can connect to universal conciousness and have an awakening. Ammonites can be used to activate kundalini currents, and with life path energies encoded within it. This card will help you to create the structure and clarity needed to uncover your soul's true path.

There is a period of renewal that you are moving through. Work with the spiral to improve the flow of life-force energy through you, which will support your cycles of death and rebirth. Surround yourself with the spiral to wind in new fresh energies into your body, to help move stagnant energy and bring ease of flow. Ammonites will convert any negative energy, stagnancy or blockages in your system into pure positivity by gently flowing in a smooth spiral flow of life-force energy. You can visualize it swirling around each cell and each strand of DNA. It is a special and gentle karmic cleansing energy that is working with you to unlock and expand in more light.

Amphibole Quartz

ELEMEMT:
Earth ▽

MEANING:
The answer is within;
listen to your inner voice

Amphibole quartz is a rare quartz crystal that is formed with the most beautiful inclusions within it. You can see them on the card, ranging from pink lithium to red hematite and yellow limonite. It is also known as Angel Phantom Quartz or Angel Wing Phantom Quartz because the mineral inclusions often appear as wispy angel wings or feather-like patterns. The colours of the inclusions can vary, appearing in white, grey, green, red or brown, depending on the minerals involved. When you gaze at it, you feel like you are pulled into the stone, and similarly the heart.

Amphibole Quartz tells us the only way is in ... stop looking outside of yourself for answers, meaning and validation. You have it all – you need to trust yourself, knowing this will sharpen your intuitive senses. Give yourself the space and time to listen to the feelings your body offers you, and the signs the spirit leaves for you.

Look within to validate. Recognize and appreciate your innate wisdom, achievements and beautiful loving qualities. Amphibole Quartz wishes to guide you on this path of living with purpose and confidence that you are embarking on. All you need to know is that nothing is beyond you, everything is achievable.

Angelite and Angelica

ELEMEMT:
Air △

MEANING:
Ask for help

On this card you see a piece of Angelite surrounded by soft white feathers – finding a feather is a sign from the angels that you are on the right path. Angelite brings courage and faith. She is a stone to hold close during adversity, and paints angelic light around you that will take you by the hand, look into your eyes with unwavering compassion and encourage you to move forward, step by step, one foot in front of the other. Visualize Angelite's gentle blue etheric energy entering your heart and crown, and call Angelica's delicate white flowers into your body to bloom around your heart. Their energy together enables you to soften and welcome change.

Their message is simple and sweet: don't struggle when you have so many around you, seen and unseen, who will help you. Reach out, call someone, ask for your angels to surround you in light now. If you feel overwhelmed, that everything is too much or going too fast, take a step into the heart and pause. Sometimes asking for help isn't easy, especially if you have grown up providing the structures you need for yourself, and independence is something you have always clung to. Remember, the angels are ready, always waiting for the wishes, hopes and prayers that you send out, but you always have to ask them for their help before they can give it.

This is not a race, it never was, nor ever has been. The path of your enlightenment stretches in front of you in all directions. There is no uphill climb, no fires to walk through, no great initiation. It is all an illusion. The path of love is infinite and you are on it – you are on it, every day, walking step by step.

Apache Tears

ELEMEMT:
Earth, Water ▽̵ ▽

MEANING:
Grief

This card took me to Superior in Arizona to visit the site of the Apache Tears legend. While connecting with the ancestors of that land, I was offered a clay peace pipe, which you can see on the card, to symbolize connection and protection in community. The Eagle flew overhead, imbuing me with energies of courage and strength as I sat with Apache Tears' messages of expressing grief. Sometimes when we are grieving it can feel like it's never-ending. Just as we get up and move forward another wave can hit us. Apache Tears hold, transmute and flow with you through your tears, and the grief of your ancestors. If you've drawn this card, it comes to you as an emotional soother, but does not stifle the tears and pain, and encourages you to feel it all and lean into the uncomfortable. After you come to the place of accepting life-shattering truths, Apache Tears shows you the breadth of your new emotional landscape.

Let Apache Tears' energy surround and hold you now, as a black glow fills your field with a lightness and gentleness you did not expect. It has the extraordinary capacity to hold emotions with no judgement. It holds its own space strongly too, knowing emotional boundaries are needed, and it does not need to be cleansed or charged. This is something we could learn from Apache Tears. It gives you the grace of "space" because you can't rush your healing – it is awkward and hard but it's necessary not to bury these things. You may be going through harder times but so much growth is coming. Everything is going to be OK, and good times are on their way.

Axinite

ELEMEMT:
Earth ▽

MEANING:
Awakening ancient past lives

For this card Axinite wanted to be painted as blades that come up, almost cutting through the sea to form mountains. These stones sing the message of finding structure and stability through ever-moving and transitional times. There is more to this than meets the eye – like the iceberg mostly hidden under the water, maybe there is a situation you are dealing with currently where it's not all as it seems. Take your time to feel into it – the whole story is not exposed yet.

The name Axinite comes from the Greek word "axina", meaning "axe", because it forms in axe-like blades, to cut away what you do not need. Axinite is encoded with much information on the spiritual laws of this universe. It accesses cosmic planes of consciousness, which not only offer you bigger-picture information on our own personal incarnations but also on Earth's evolutionary process. As you drew this card, these are now offered to you. Axinite likes to ground and hold the physical body through change and give you the insight and ability to look to the great balance and flow of the universe and cosmos and your place in it.

Axinite energy comes through the back and holds your spine and physical body deeply, encasing you in a strong nurturing vibration. It wishes to hold your core, your skeletal structure and spine, and its energy is all about supporting the physical body through change and transformation as it calls forward the past lives in your cellular memory to witness the releases you are having to enable your soul's growth. Change is growth; whether you view it as positive or negative, it is all growth.

One of Axenite's gifts is to bring forward your past memories to view them, and it can do this with many lives at once. It can help you merge and collapse many timelines, so call its energy in with care to help you support your growth and change. It will aid you in letting go the energies that do not serve you or your highest and greatest good.

Beech Pod

ELEMEMT:
Earth ▽

MEANING:
Wishes granted

This card has a focus of three beech seed pods, which are "wishes" for you to make and manifest with the energies of the faery keepers and the beech tree; they are the treasure and the ways to manifest your hopes, dreams and wishes.

The Beech tree is the queen of the forest. Alongside her king, the Oak, she upholds the faery energies, the passageways into the Earth, sending the messages through her roots where they are carried by the winds into the roots and systems of all around her. If you draw this card, the soil will become saturated with your loving intent and wishes, carried further down to the inner realms where they are listened to. If you are looking for wishes to be granted, cast your hopes and dreams into the Beech seed pod and scatter them onto the Earth in thanks. Beech is known to offer protection and nourishment, as she fans her branches out into a broad canopy that is useful for shelter. People once relied upon her Beech Pods to keep themselves from starvation, and collecting them helped strengthen the bonds between the community or clans.

The Beech Pod's energy helps you get closer to your ancestors and their knowledge passed down through time and stories stored deep within, like the potential stored in the pod that a Beech tree has put out.

Make a wish, focus your intent now on what you heart wants to create, plant it in light in the Beech Pod and say a simple prayer to the Earth as you send it down to it through the roots of the Beech. There are many elemental friends watching over you, ready to help this wish bloom.

Blue Heron

ELEMEMT:
Water, Earth, Air
▽ ▽△

MEANING:
Patience; transformation; messenger

This Heron appears in blue flames of truth. It can constantly set itself on fire, transforming without fear, holding the same patient look on its face as if it were waiting poised for a fish. Nothing phases the Heron, and it stands still, quiet and confident in its conviction to change and endless transformation. Transformation is happening in every moment all around us on a cellular level. If you drew this card, the Heron shows you how simple it can be if you are patient and have faith that the universe is working in your favour, even if things are not happening as quickly as you would like.

The Heron transcends three elements: Water, Earth and Air. It is a messenger of truth and integrity, whose lack of grounding allows it to travel with ease through the in-between states, the heavens and the underworld to bring you lessons of life and birth. It teaches the valuable viewpoints of patience, self-reliance and the ways to create balance within. Its lesson is one of longevity. It shows us what commitment looks like and how to show up for ourselves and each other with a balanced, loving viewpoint on the situation.

Carnelian

ELEMEMT:
Fire △

MEANING:
Sacred rage

Carnelian wanted to be painted emerging from a woman's yoni as a fiery portal of power: of rage, grief and anger. A wolf sits on either side, representing the light and dark within. These mother wolves ask you to surrender and trust their support: call on them as heart gatekeepers to guide you through release. This is a serious card and it holds a really strong message of self-expression: it is a time to tap into and express repressed feelings, and many of these are stored in the wombspace.

Carnelian is a stone of the triple goddess. When working with her, the spirit of the goddess comes through, and brings us the unified balance of the maiden, the mother and the crone. Carnelian's gift is one of love, warmth and passion that unites sovereign power within you. The fire she brings to your sacral chakra, and your womb, if you have one, is not overpowering. It's a gentle flame stirring passion, sexuality, your divine feminine to stand tall, fully embodied. Her energy is all wise woman, who knows who she is, and knows with faith what she is here to offer, and she imbues these qualities within you.

Carnelian's darker shades also bring a masculine energy in balance and heal traumas to the sexual organs, both from this life and past lives. The lighter shades of this crystal, with golden tones, bring a reminder of the lightness of life, a golden ray that lifts us emotionally when facing this deep work. It is full of life-force energy and will boost yours! Its warmth is also felt in the throat chakra, where it brings forward your voice, whether that's individual or as a community. The womb and throat are closely interwoven, and Carnelian will support the release of the voice, helping you to create womb space so you can connect with your songs. She is the singer's stone.

When we empty ourselves, we make room for the new, carving space to let the sacred rage bubble up, whether you find a quiet spot with a big pillow to vent into, or smash or thrash, it can be extremely cathartic. Tune into your primal energy, letting out a roar, or howl like a wolf. Make noise and take up space.

Chalcedony Navel Stone

ELEMEMT:
Water ▽

MEANING:
Voicing the unspoken

Chalcedony is sometimes called the "Navel Stone" because working with Chalcedony brings your focus to your navel, and it revealed to me a beautiful umbilical cord of golden light to source energy from. The stone showed me a baby in the womb connected to Source and receiving its golden life-force energy, and it wanted this replicated on its card. The card could be representative of you in your mother's womb, invoking feelings of connection or nourishment. It asks you to bring all your awareness to your solar plexus, or navel, right now. It works on the emotional layer of the body as a cleanser. There is unspoken pain, anger and worry that needs to surface. Chalcedony holds that space for the silenced and unspoken voices to rise from the belly. It befriends anguish, strolling arm and arm with it, soothing and holding it.

When connecting with its spiralling energy in your navel, you might be surprised at how instantly the voices of anger or grief arise: Chalcedony's medicine is fast and powerful. In the same breath it will bring a wave of calm through the nervous system as it suppresses the fight-or-flight response, to remind you that you are safe. You do not have to hide, step out of your body or close down. It will stretch and open the solar plexus so that these negative feelings can just flow from you – all you have to do is observe it and let it go.

After Chalcedony's cleansing action comes re-balancing of the emotions, then the burst of motherly love. It offers the image of an umbilical cord, and asks you to connect with the umbilical cord you had in your mother's womb, feeling its golden light and allowing the love from your mother to flow through you now. Fostering maternal instincts, Chalcedony is a stone for the mothers and those moving through a maiden to a mother phase. She is a goddess stone, connected in all ways to the divine mother and her nourishing energy, which is sweet honey love for the soul.

To feel Chalcedony's cleansing, follow these steps. Take some breaths into your solar plexus, expanding your belly as full as it can go, feel into this centre and ask your body:

How does my body feel?
What emotions do I need to tend to?

Sometimes we need to dig deeper, so ask yourself the same questions again, as you peel back the layers. May the sweet motherly love of Chalcedony be with you, infusing your solar plexus with golden healing light.

Covellite

ELEMEMT:
Air △

MEANING:
Past-life healing;
Akashic field

Covellite wished to be painted in a very witchy way, to bring empowerment back to the women who have been persecuted for being powerful. It showed me a cauldron overflowing with its blue energies, swirling magically around to take the form of a piece of covellite.

An extremely rare copper-based stone, covellite is a powerful talisman for protection, change and transformation. If this crystal's energy has been drawn to you, it's asking you to focus on your third eye chakra: cleansing, expanding and unlocking it with its swirling blue metallic energy. It will take you first through that chakra, where its energy fills up and unlocks and restores psychic gifts of sight. Covellite pulls forward any past-life wounds and scar imprints on the body to heal them. It specifically connects us to the collective wounds of the sisterhood, to explore and heal "witch" wounds within and around. It offers a mystic, wise energy that will whisper through the darkness of your dreams and ask you to journey with it through the flames of your heart to receive the ultimate alchemical initiations of the heart.

There is an opportunity for an Akashic clearing at this time if you hold the intent for this. The Akashic field, or Akasha, is the field of energy where the records of our lives on Earth are stored. The stone will help you to open, pull forward and heal wounds that appear in your aura and the psychic imprints that are left of any emotional fragmentation form multiple timelines at once. It is a very powerful past-life healer, as it aligns you completely with the Akashic field of all your past-life records.

Crow and Black Moonstone

ELEMEMT:
Air △

MEANING:
Witness; reflect; observe

This card is an invitation to journey into yourself with the crow and black moonstone.

The crow is the watcher of the winds, the witness of light and dark, a record keeper of old who records the Earth's transitions. She picks up the red thread of the ancestors and honours it: the thread that they have woven through the stories of their life. This thread forges a deep connection with the past. She calls you to the old ways and encourages you to listen to the stories of your ancestral land.

She does not judge, she does not pressure, poke or question. She is silent and offers endless perspectives, and is ready to stand by and witness all of your facets and aspects. When areas of doubt and fear arise, look at them through the eyes of the crow, and you will find answers through the shadows you need to greet. She is a master shadow weaver: with her, you are in good hands. She will support you in transmuting fear. Her sharp sounds will pierce your inner eye and she offers a shrill wake-up call, awakening the senses, honing and fine tuning your psychic skills.

She asks:

What do you need to bring focus to at this moment?

Have you been too much of a bystander in your own story recently? Not taking the reins, allowing yourself to be led? Then it's time to take up the thread for yourself and take control of your narrative. The crow comes at the close of a cycle to record and witness.

After this time of regeneration, action and creation are needed.

Ask her:

Grandmother Crow, what are you witnessing in me at this time? What must I see in myself?

Black Moonstone is as ancient as the moon itself. It reflects the energies of the dark moon, the last visible crescent of a waning moon, to you at this time. As the crow spirit brings the close of a cycle that has run its course, so does dark moon energy of Black Moonstone. The guardian of the shadows, it is full of mystery and allows you to travel inward without judgement. Black Moonstone is a wisdom keeper for the old Earth crone mothers, where stillness and wisdom reigns. It provides that void to rest and reflect.

Desert Rose Selenite

ELEMEMT:
Earth, Air ▽ △

MEANING:
Building foundations for security and safety

Desert Rose Selenite wanted to be painting "whipping up a storm", surrounded by a vortex of air, swirling, moving and clearing energies. This is the very nature of how this stone is formed – over time sand becomes embedded within Selenite blades with the action of wind, and the addition of water makes it form the rosette formation it is known for.

The vortex depicted on this card is showing you that there is movement around you, and you need to root down to create strong foundations and stability to keep from being swept up in it. Focus on what is important.

Desert Rose Selenite is a builder stone, creating strong foundations of security and stability in the root chakra and up to the sacral, where it supports work on your self-esteem and self-worth. Its energy encourages you to give yourself "permission" right now to release painful trapped emotions such as grief, anger and confusion. It asks you to bring focus to ancestral patterns that need to be healed and released from the spine, as it is one of the best crystals for clearing congested energies or negativity from the physical and etheric bodies. It unbinds, releases and removes emotional trauma from the sacral chakra and lower back too. This card reminds you that you have power – stand in it and don't let the expectations of others hold you back or determine your own expectations of yourself.

Desert Rose Selenite's energy is full of movement and air, with a very potent cleansing action. It calls small whirlpools of energy in the body to spin up and clear anything that does not belong. It then sweeps in a calm clarity after the release, bringing self-assurance in its wake. The stone gives you the courage to face your fears, and do the things you know you need to do.

This stone works closely with the planetary stargate on Andromeda, anchoring the higher frequencies into the Earth through the capital of inner Earth, Agartha.

Working with it aligns you to many ancient earth dragon tribes and sand dragons who come in to support your soul's evolution and expansion. It's a stone for the womb augmentation (the process of making something bigger or greater). In doing this it opens you up to the greater mysteries of the cosmos and allows the Earth to move through you. This stone marries you to the Earth and the stars.

Desert Rose Selenite speaks:

"The most sacred work we can do is to take ancient pain and transform it into acts of love."

Dragonfly Spirit and Rose Quartz

ELEMEMT:
Air, Water △▽

MEANING:
Love and freedom

Dipping and diving into the depths of the heart, the Dragonfly is a master weaver of frequency, navigating the slipstreams, darting through the unknown with you. If you drew this card, she will weave new pathways into being within you, waking up your heart up to more love, more possibilities and freedom. Hers is a dance of beauty, delicacy and companionship. The codes of light the Dragonfly offers you move through its beating wings through the crown chakra and into the heart. If you are blessed to have one land on you, receive its glistening love like a rainbow.

Rose Quartz is the ultimate heart companion, a stone some people overlook as it's just so abundant in the Earth, but it is always there for you. If you drew this card, you are going through a tough transition, and it offers the gentleness and tender holding needed as you navigate this time of heart opening, coming to help take away the rawness and pain, reminding the heart that it is OK. Her light is one of ease and grace: she doesn't push you, but stands back to hold you when you most need it, giving a pink ray of divine love to wrap around yourself. You can turn to Rose Quartz over and over again.

Eudialyte and Pine

ELEMEMT:
Earth, Water ▽ ▽

MEANING:
Protective medicine of the Sámi people

The energies of this stone showed how it wished to be painted – with a Sámi Elder, her drum and a reindeer from her herd, and a piece of Eudialyte between its antlers. Eudialyte is a journey stone and companion on adventures of expansion. Offering universal emotional support, if you drew this card it brings you a calm and stabilizing voice through emotional ups and downs. It will support your heart and reawaken passion, calming tension in relationships and enhancing communication, helping you to reconnect to your loved ones spiritually, emotionally and physically.

The ancestral guardians of this stone, the Sámi people of the arctic regions of Norway, Sweden and Finland, used pine for many purposes including as food and medicine. Pine brings peace to the fractured feelings that Eudialyte uncovers, and helps you to release these feelings. Together they will surround you in their glow to bring higher perspective to the journey you are on. You may be starting something new, embodying a new way of being, creating something or embarking on a new adventure or journey. Pine's energy offers strength and stability, asking you to trust your instincts and stay focused on your journey. This card signals a strong support system is dropping in for you through the voices of your ancestors. Lean into them: they will show you the way. Light a candle to honour them and say a prayer to them in gratitude.

Faden Quartz and Tansy

ELEMEMT:
Earth, Air ▽ △

MEANING:
Push through the uncomfortable

As some of the oldest quartz that's ever been uncovered, Faden Quartz contains ancient Earth energies at its core. You can see on the card that it is a thread of pure light, frozen in time. Our lightbodies are reflected back at us through it, and become a pure core of light. This presents us with the perfect opportunity to look at our growth. Allow Faden Quartz's light to move through you so you can achieve the peace and clarity you need now.

Faden Quartz is a stone of growth and change. It was given the name "Faden", meaning "thread" in German, due to its formation, as it threads itself in between rocks that have experienced major Earth shifts that broke them apart. Faden has an amazing ability to repair and continue to grow through extreme change and pressure, and this helps you to analyze your own personal growth.

Tansy's energy is wildly free, encouraging you to dream, to dare, to want and to hope for something different. She is an energy that everyone needs in their life to help them embrace change, hovering around the ears and the crown, kissing your temples, letting you know that life is for living. She lifts light into the upper chakras so you can shed unwanted mental manipulation. Being the change in your life is never easy, especially when those around you and your own thoughts challenge you.

Take a moment to still your energy with your breath, coming back to your core, your heart. Visualize yourself in a field of vibrant yellow Tansy, every small flower bursting with love and songs for you. You allow yourself to lie down and feel them begin to grow around you, creating a cradle of yellow light in the places around you that need to feel held. Welcome their energy into your body, and allow it to travel to where it needs to be.

As you breathe into your spine, you begin to feel it lengthening and expanding until it crystalizes like the Faden Quartz on this card. This core of liquid light radiates through your being now, travelling with ease and grace exactly where it needs to be.

Flint

ELEMEMT:
Earth ▽

MEANING:
Detach and release

Flint comes in various shades of brown, grey and blue. It's an abundant stone you can often see scattered across fields and pathways, and on this card it is surrounded by golden light language. Flint's voice is very direct and knowing, softening the more you speak to it. Not afraid to offend or upset, it speaks directly with a deep love for the Earth that is woven through its field. Sometimes we need a firm voice to guide us when we are unsure. Holding the Flint on this card, Flint's voice will show you the footprints of the ancestors that walked before you. Your ancestors' sacrifice created the foundations for you and where we are now, just as you will continue to live, love and sacrifice for the future.

Flint asks: what are you ready to sacrifice or let go of to move forward? Sometimes an offering of love is needed to give to the Earth, ancestors and the elementals to show your willingness and readiness.

Open your eyes to the cycles of rebirth that you and the Earth are moving through. You are resurrecting yourself over and over every day, in every moment with every breath. You are a whole new person each day, with hope and promise ahead. Don't cling too tightly to the past – instead, move with the new energies around you.

Who do you want to be today?
What do you wish to feel?
How do you wish to make others feel?

Breathe with the Earth and bring your heart into alignment with her. Call your mind to the Earth and notice the many millions of footsteps scattered across her surface. Many have walked before you, and many will continue after you. You become part of the music score of this planetary song that is built on the bones, songs and stories of the ancestors that pepper the Earth and sweeten the soil. Surrender to the never-ending spiral, knowing that nothing is permanent, everything is sacred and that you are a walking miracle and a mystery. Tend to the sacred in you. Because there is no one, or nothing more sacred than you.

Fluorite

ELEMEMT:
Air, Water △ ▽

MEANING:
Harness the power of your mind

Fluorite is known as one of the most colourful minerals in the world, coming in a variety of colours from green to purple to yellow and blue. For this card it wanted to show off its colour and be painted as Rainbow Fluorite, to reflect beauty, brightness and your exquisite colours back to you. You are as beautiful as Rainbow Fluorite.

This extraordinary creation of nature is known as the genius stone, as it interacts with the human mind like no other, helping you reach a higher state of mental awareness and clarity. It wishes you to work with its energy to learn, grow and expand at this time. It will help you deal with complex issues by sending charges through your brain cells. Drawing in more life-force energy, it encourages both hemispheres of your brain to work in a harmonious balance.

Fluorite is my number one focus stone, a stone of action and clearing the way, heralding a time for you to harness the power of your mind through creativity and imagination. If you have an idea, goal or dream, it's time to bring it fully into this reality. Sing your wishes into existence with Fluorite and plant them into the Earth. Fluorite is not known to be a manifesting stone to create your desired future or outcome, but at this time its momentum of energy can bring clarity to what you want and help you weed out what you don't. It focuses on "needs" more than "wants" and will help you visualize the end goal and achieve that, with a boost to positive outlooks in all areas of your life.

Bringing all-around empowerment, Fluorite wants to work with you to dissolve confusion and bring more peace to any destructive behaviour patterns that may be holding you back. It assists you in overcoming limiting beliefs in yourself and comparison with others. But, despite this, I feel Fluorite's greatest gift is its ability to bring you into alignment with the law of one: we are all interconnected, something we need to remind ourselves of regularly for higher perspective.

Himalayan Quartz

ELEMEMT:
Air △

MEANING:
Realizations

You are wanted
You are needed
You are a divine spark calling others home with you,
Like a lighthouse.

Himalayan Quartz painted the image of a lighthouse, moored on crystallized rocks in the ocean, with its pure brilliant light calling you home, guiding you and showing you the way. New pathways are opening for you and you will find the answers you need shortly. Just be one with and receptive to the signs from the spirit. Look for the rainbows in the storm.

Himalayan Quartz asks you to come home to it – don't let the pain that ripples through you be the reason you close yourself off. Let its energies help you open. Find the unloved parts of you that need to be resurrected in its light and hold yourself in love. Let go of old patterns, behaviours and thoughts. You are not seeing clearly right now because you are in your head. Call back your energies and sit in your heart. Now is not the time to be making any big decisions or spontaneous choices, it's a time to be still and feel. You will come into the heart and trust yourself. Your energy is busy and scattered and needs to be called home.

Nothing is lost, everything is going to be alright. There is no roadmap through the heart: you will take different paths and routes but it will always lead you to the perfect destination. Sometimes it will take longer than you imagined because the light that carries you forward gets lost in the fog of fear.

Within Himalayan Quartz is a divine force, a strong light that you can call on to guide you. It is a lantern to light the way forward through your heart healing; its energy will drive you through the darker places within with confidence – when a light shines so bright it dazzles all around it. Through the journey with its energy you will realize that it is not the stone that is this light, but you.

Himalayan Quartz comes to you to help you recognize your light, your abilities and your gifts, to help you heal and move on, clearing your crown to release unloving thoughts and negativity toward yourself and calming the mind. These energies are encoded in the card and if you gaze at it, it will support your crown to help you find your way home to your heart.

Lemurian Crystal

ELEMEMT:
Earth, Air ▽ △

MEANING:
Motherline healing;
cycle breaker

This card shows a Lemurian crystalline city of light, with a doorway into the crystal temple. Lemurian Crystals invite you into their inner chambers. They ask you to mother and hold yourself tenderly at this time; gentleness is needed with big emotions, grace is needed to carry you through the ever-changing landscape of your heart.

Lemurian Crystals are a higher vibration of quartz that were carried to many points of the world and hidden for when humanity is ready. They are ascension keys of light, like all quartz, but they have a specific mission to open and activate deeper chambers of the heart. This card's medicine is making you aware of the great healing and movement that's happening on your motherline, the line of women who came before you. It's either bringing focus to what you need to do, or reminding you that you're doing it, living through it and are a cycle breaker.

Lemurian crystals are heart-awakening stones – they are here to take us deeper into our hearts, and just like our hearts, they tell me they have many chambers within to explore. It is important when working with a lemurian crystal that you take yourself inside the crystal to explore and receive.

As stones of the divine mother, Lemurian crystals are here to help us awaken to the shekinah flow of life (the feminine flow of energy through the spine). They will teach you of the divinity of your soul and help you heal raw emotional themes around abandonment by our mother. This is something that many of us lightworkers carry through the ages within our ancestry.

Limestone Guardians

ELEMEMT:
Earth ▽

MEANING:
Record keepers; reviewing choices and pathways

This card shows West Kennet Long Barrow, part of the Avebury complex; these grandmother stones evoke the messages of limestone, and they watch and record the events of time and the stories of the ancestors for you to tune into. You will notice three swallow guardians swooping past – a message of change and luck.

Limestone is a sedimentary rock containing animal shells and corals that forms in shallow, calm and warm waters. Many of the sacred sites of the world are built using some limestone, including the pyramids of Egypt, the step pyramid of Chichén Itzá, the Acropolis in Athens and the Colosseum in Rome. In Britain, some of the giants at Avebury and West Kennet Long Barrow are made up of limestone.

This rock captures the voices of those who have spoken in and around it, those who have climbed within its caves, sung to it in thanks or climbed its dizzying heights. Limestone is happy to share its recordings, if you place your hand on it and ask: it has a wealth of healing information locked within waiting to be shared

It also enhances purification and healing with a quiet, steady, grounding energy that finds you now, and says:

"You too are a crystalline record keeper: everything is recorded within your cells. I stand still observing, never able to change or affect anything that passes. I ask that you take the role of observer more deeply. Try not to attach too much to thoughts and actions, and just observe them like I do."

This card draws on the energies of the sacred limestone sites.

Magnetite

ELEMEMT:
Earth ▽

MEANING:
*Energetic attunements; clear
direction; expansion*

Magnetite is a very powerful stone. Like its name suggests it is magnetic and attracts and magnetizes strong energy currents to flow through you. It wished to be painted surrounding the Earth, showing how it heals the Earth's blocked energy points, and it also reflects this with you. It asks you to breathe into your body and feel it in places and spaces within you that feel heavy and need loosening up with light and movement. Do not neglect to check in with your body as much as you can at this time. As the Earth is moving through a time of great energetic change, so are you, and you need to keep everything flowing and moving as best you can. This is a reminder to take care of your physical self as well as your energetic body. Your human body is the house of your soul, your eyes the windows: care for your body and mind at this time and be gentle on yourself.

Magnetite works on the energy centres of the body, the meridians (in traditional Chinese medicine, meridians are channels that form a network in the body, through which chi or vital energy flows) and magnetic field, balancing and waking up dormant energy pathways. It has strong energy of harmony and Earth healing. This energy will travel to the point of disturbed energy in your body or the Earth and will clear this disturbance to make way for new energies.

Magnetite just wants to fill you up with the Earth and support all areas of expansion in your life. It instantly attunes to the Earth's electro-magnetic field to support all realignment. Providing a highly effective spiritual grounding cord into the Earth, it aligns and activates all chakras, especially the root, and fills them with an abundance of Earth energy.

With this card, you are creating a new template for yourself, your loved ones and your community. There is a strong and clear resonance rippling through your energetic field for all to feel: you're magnetic too, and many things including opportunities, abundance, people and animals will be drawn to you. All the healing work you have done is coming to fruition, so take time to enjoy it.

Moqui Marbles

ELEMEMT:
Earth ▽

MEANING:
More balance needed

Moqui Marbles wished to be painted in the card on golden scales showing the balance they hold. This is something that they promote through all levels of the physical, mental, emotional and spiritual. They ask you to bring awareness to the areas of your life that you could bring more balance to. The card holds the number six, which is an angel number guiding us to cultivate a balance between the material and spirit worlds.

Moqui Marbles are found in pairs that possess female and male energies. The female Moqui Marble is smooth and the male is more textured. It is this balance of yin and yang energies that makes them excellent companions in energy work and spiritual development, as they cleanse, ground and align the chakras.

Moqui Marbles are a gift from the Earth to rebalance all parts of us. If this card has shown up in your reading, it is asking you to bring more balance into your life where possible. Perhaps you need more work–life balance; there is a time to do and a time to rest, which is it for you now? Perhaps you have been very much in masculine mode recently, constantly striving and doing things, and you are being asked to rest and conserve more energy. Feel into it as you ask yourself, your heart and your body: where can I bring balance?

Moqui Marbles have an electro-magnetic energy, with each having both a positive and negative side. Working with a pair, one female and one masculine held in each hand brings harmony to all systems of your body. They work to take excess energy down from the root to be discharged at your earth star chakra, the perfect companion after spiritual development to run off excess energies and anchor into the Earth grids more substantially.

Nuummite

ELEMEMT:
Fire $\triangle$

MEANING:
Safe spaces; emotional security; dragon energy,

Nummite draws the fiery energies from the Earth and combines the elements of a storm with this strong connection to wild nature energies. It's a magician's stone, connected closely to elemental magic. It sparks action and asks you to walk the path truest to you, to show the way and to have courage and belief in yourself.

You can see from the flecks of gold and bronze that shimmer through its black surface that it's a stone calling you in to look beyond and deeper. With this stone a blue dragon from Sirius flew in as a guardian, and this playful galactic creature nurtures hope and calls you to action, to imbue within you the strength and courage you need to walk the path of your truest and most heart-aligned expression. This is what Nummite wishes to guide you toward.

Nuummite is one of the oldest minerals on the planet, formed over three billion years ago from volcanic origins. Nuummite facilitates the journeying into other worlds to retrieve lost souls and soul fragments. It draws out negative energies, mental imprints, curses and implants from outside sources. For those who have misused power in the past, this stone helps you do the emotional work so that you can view it from a different perspective to be able to release the guilt, shame or fear easier. This makes it a fierce protector stone banishing negative energies, manipulation, environmental pollutants and sorcery.

Nuummite is also a masculine stone. Known as the sorcerer's stone, it teaches the wisdom of the alchemists. Their wisdom is stored within: pure elemental alchemy that deepens our connection to the natural world, and its wild and raw elemental powers.

Merlin calls this stone the dragon whistle, because it calls forward dragon tribes of vast power. Offering incredible grounding support and boosting life-force energy when worked with or worn, its strong electro-magnetic field aligns your subtle energy bodies and strengthens your aura.

Calling the medicine of this card to you is bringing your dragon tribes to rally around you for extra transmuting and protection. You are moving through periods of intense healing and reflection. Nuummite's energy wishes to take you into the void to witness the emotional wounds surfacing in you, helping you release control. Do not let your fears become so powerful that they control you.

Pietersite and Animal Guides

ELEMEMT:
Earth, Air ▽ △

MEANING:
Shapeshifter powers to offer greater perspective

This card brings the spirit of the animals to you, especially the big cats. It takes you on a journey to connect with the animal kingdom where they can teach us so much about this Earth. The black void space represents the wisdom we can find in the silence.

Pietersite is a very shamanic stone, assisting us in inter-dimensional travel. It is made up of a collection of Hawk's Eye, Tiger's eye and Blue Tiger's Eye. So the spirit of the animals live in its very makeup. It is a very rare stone with potent energy to bring change and activate your mental field. This stone has the ability to take you to a calm state in meditation where you can shapeshift into the animal guides to see things through their eyes, offering the great gift of higher perspective.

This card holds the energies of all of the animal kingdom. Gaze softly at it and close your eyes, let the energies of the stone and the darkness weave in around you, holding you. When you are ready, call forward an animal guide to steer your heart at this time. Let the animal expand through your heart until it fills your body and attunes its energies, feelings and thoughts through you, sharing consciousness. It has so much to teach you. Be still and listen, allow it to guide you fully.

It is time to pause and be more perceptive to your environment and those around you. Step back and take a look at what is in ebb and flow. There are a great many and vast things that affect our inner tides, you are stuck in your own inner world and need to look to the cause and effect, the relationship between two events or a situation that caused the other. What was the initiating event that brought you to this place, and the effect of that on you and your family, your friends and your community? It's important to look at how this situation not only affects you but those close to you, and how you can focus on them at this time. Come out of the "I" and into the "we" and the "us".

Pink Aragonite

ELEMEMT:
Water $\triangledown$

MEANING:
Patience and trust;
healing relationships

Trust the process, the rest will follow.

Pink Aragonite is a fairly uncommon crystal. It is found in oxidized zones of ore deposits, in caves as stalactites and near hot springs. Its bubble-gum pink colours range from pale to bright magenta, as you can see on the card, which comes from an inclusion of cobalt. Often found in Argentina and China, they can be discovered banded with white calcite, which forms beautiful stripes that you can work with to take you through to the layers of your heart.

This stone sings of tenderness and love that is so sweet and gentle that it softens you. Its energy works to align with the signature vibration of the heart, flexible in nature, bringing flow to the hidden spaces and the root of the problem that lies in the most hidden depths of your heart.

Pink Aragonite is full of so much love that it can't help but inspire you to love yourself more. Its love is unconditional, and when you love yourself more your heart shines brighter and showers those around you in love. It asks you if there are relationships around you that need some work. Its pink light brings tolerance, trust and understanding so that you can experience deeper, more fulfilling and healthier relationships with yourself and others.

Polychrome Jasper

ELEMEMT:
Earth, Fire ▽△

MEANING:
New pathways; new becomes old; old becomes new

Polychrome Jasper wished to be painted whimsically for this card – it showed a magical landscape that it likened to Earth, full of warm orange, brown and teal tones, with a golden pathway leading through the centre to a glorious new beginning. It sings that this is your future, highest timelines are merging for you, bring new beginnings and new opportunities. Luck is with you! This stone's energy brings the reminder that anything is possible and that you truly are the shaper of your reality. Sometimes we need the reminder.

Polychrome Jasper, also known as desert jasper, is a slow and steady ancient Earth energy. It was recently discovered in Madagascar in 2008 when digging for highly sought-after Ocean Jasper. This Jasper speaks of attention to detail: do not miss the signs that are all around you, and take notice of the synchronicities that nudge and can direct you if you choose to see them. Kundalini is the sexual energy stored at the base of our spine, sometimes referred to as shakti. Both men and women have it, and when you work with that energy and bring it consciously up the spine to the crown you can connect to universal consciousness and have an awakening. As a kundalini activator, it helps you face growth and changes in your life, and who better to walk this new path with? Polychrome Jasper comes to help you open up to new pathways as they are around you, and it clears energy blockages in the way, enabling rebirth and transformation. It offers steady, stable energy that grounds you in your choices.

In the quantum realm there are thousands of possibilities, and then there is the ability you have to create new pathways. You can recycle energies – what was old can become new with fresh eyes, an energy shift and an expanded mind. Do not be so fast to dismiss. Just as old can become new, new can become old very fast. In this world the fast pace pushes us toward instant gratification, so explore the options you have in more depth, and take your time to explore all the possibilities because you will find there are more than you realize open to you at this time.

Rhodochrosite

ELEMEMT:
Water ▽

MEANING:
Release doubt and pain

When working with the medicine of Rhodochrosite, it offered me the beautiful image of a vibrant red rose opening in the heart, a connection to Mary Magdalene's energy, as I wrote this card in the south of France while visiting her sacred caves in the mountains. The rose holds the highest "love" vibration of all the flowers and offers you the vision of red roses blooming in your heart now.

Rhodochrosite teaches us how to love. It can help you see what your heart desires, and what it truly needs. It shows us how simplicity is everything – in that space of simplicity we have fewer distractions of the ego – and it asks you to look inward with calm focus, to locate the pain you didn't know you were carrying, the emotions you have kept locked, hidden and buried.

This stone sees all of you, and loves all of you, and helps you move through sadness, grief, anxiety or anger, washing through it to bring quiet understanding and emotional respite, which helps you find clarity on situations sooner. It is not the pain It will erase, just the understanding and feelings around the reasons why.

Celebrate the now; find solace in reflection and quiet moments. Breathe into your heart with Rhodochrosite and create space within your body to smile at the goodness and sweetness of life, for the grief and pain are reminders to live, they are reflections of love.

Rose and Pink Opal

ELEMEMT:
Water $\triangledown$

MEANING:
Grace

Pink Opal's energy calls forward heart opening. It is known as the stone of spiritual awakening, hopefulness, renewal and growth. A sweet feminine energy, it enhances the divine mother within you and strengthens your sacred connection to the creator energies within your heart and womb, a gift to help ease any process of change. It will massage the heart to gently open and activate while keeping you grounded. Even the hardest of hearts can soften, even the most difficult challenges can be overcome. Those going through the pain of separation can still find wholeness in the divine dispensation of grace and softening of open hearts that Pink Opal can offer.

Place the pink Rose on the card deep within the walls of your womb and call in the soft pink flow of Pink Opal to show you your beauty. Offer yourself the gift of grace today, or ask yourself who you can offer grace to. Lay the Rose down at the altar of your heart and be one with the eternal flow of grace as it moves like a glistening diamond river into your deepest heart chambers. Its light moves through the darkness toward you, your heart a lighthouse calling out for it; let compassion calm any storms.

You are doing the best you can to show yourself compassion. Take a breath and let go of the hold fear has. This is a reminder that everything is in perfect divine flow for you.

Ruby and Scorpion

ELEMEMT:
Water, Fire ▽△

MEANING:
*Unwavering love
and devotion*

This Scorpion wished to be painted in the darkness holding a polished glowing Ruby between its pincers, which symbolizes retrieving the light, and being the light. It sings the song of "emergence": you are emerging from something hard, and you have done a beautiful job of navigating the tough nature of the challenge. Acknowledge this and find grace in knowing that you did your best and that's enough. The polished Ruby shines a light on your soul and reflects this light at you to remind you of your beauty and inner wisdom. The rough hexagonal ruby holds many triangular "record keeper" markings that symbolize past-life trauma has healed, so give yourself space to sit with this and discover what it means to you.

Rubies ooze sensuality, passion and fire. The Ruby and Scorpion is such an activating card, marking a complete overhaul and/or re-structuring of your lower chakras in turn. If you draw this card, a process of emptying has happened to re-stabilize and re-ground your lower chakras with a higher vibration. You have moved through the harder times, and ease and grace flows through your waters now.

According to Vedic astrology, the Ruby is a gemstone of the sun, a symbol of Ra, creation, life force and the soul of the cosmic body. Ruby is also associated with royalty and love, and the god Eros, as it is a powerful heart opener and activator, carrying the vibration of divine love to you now, as you wade the watery depths of this path. Ruby's energy is slow, decisive and strong. Growing and spreading its light through your lower chakras and lightbody, it offers you the visual of a ruby sun rising at your root. It is a stone that inspires passion, asking to be teamed with the depths of Scorpio. These serve as a good team, supporting the final phases of transformation. The energies of the Ruby and scorpion transmute with a sharp and quick action to support you as you receive expansion.

The Scorpion has the ability as a guide to take you down into the depths and dance with the fragility of life and death. The ancient Egyptians revered the Scorpion spirit as a potent guardian for the souls moving from one world to the next. From a shamanic point of view the Scorpion was a spirit guide that created a change or shift in consciousness for the one it appeared to.

Sea Coal

ELEMEMT:
Water, Fire ▽△

MEANING:
Progress; divine order;
a new cycle

Sea Coal speaks:

> *"Life can flourish in the hardest, most extreme*
> *environments, and if it can flourish there so can you."*

Sea Coal sits proudly in the centre of this card, invoking the energies of the tides crashing on the shore beneath it. Coal is one of the most ancient energy resources our Earth holds. It is a sedimentary rock, formed over millions of years from the remains of plant matter such as ferns that died in swamp lands. It is mostly made of carbon, which is abundant on Earth and is the chemical backbone of life, the food that sustains us and provides energy. Coal speaks of the Earth's progress, its origin stories and root races – the first humans on Earth. If you drew this card, it asks you to focus on your progress for a moment, to help you re-group and regain focus and clarity on where you are heading. What you are building comes from the hallowed grounds your ancestors laid, and you continue to build and create healing templates for future generations. Change is coming, but it takes commitment and dedication. Coal is a reminder that you signed up to this.

Coal holds in its energy field the energetic power of the Earth from when the Coal was formed. So who better to understand the flow state of the universe and divine order? With Coal you can trust the natural order and surrender to the universal flow – everything is happening for your highest good, even if you cannot understand it at the time. It is a teacher stone, understanding the balance of work and play, when to take action and when to rest, knowing that even as you rest so much is going on beneath the surface.

On a practical level, Coal asks us to look at our environment. It's very aware of electro-magnetic disturbance, so ask yourself how environmental frequencies are affecting you and your energy field right now, both positively and negatively. If you feel you are in a space of frequency disturbance, consider getting out in nature to cleanse and refresh your lightbody.

Sedona Red Rock

ELEMEMT:
Earth ▽

MEANING:
*You're beautiful and perfect
exactly as you are*

*Your life is a tapestry,
Beauty woven into every thread
The tapestry is woven across lives and inter-dimensional
plane
Your legacy is love
Each thread of love is woven into the ether.*
Kachina Woman

Sedona Red Rock speaks to you of the beauty within. Also known as the the Kachina Woman, she is painted on this card, and the words about the tapestry above came to me as I sat with her. To connect with her energies, remember that the beauty you see around you is a reflection of the beauty within you. On this card you will see a coyote, known as the trickster – his medicine shows us that when something is hurtful it's actually a healing lesson. He came in to stand by my side as I journeyed with the energies of the Arizona landscape.

For centuries, Native American tribes considered the Red Rocks in Arizona sacred. They would travel to the stones to collect crystals and plants to work with the vortex energies there for their journeying and prayers. I wrote this card at the Kachina Woman rock at Boynton Canyon vortex in Sedona, a sacred site of the Hopi Nation. She is a sacred protector to their people and a reminder of their teachings. When I sat with my back against the rock she said to me: "You are pregnant with the universe", a sentiment I echo to you now, dear friend.

Kachina Woman refers to herself as a birthing stone, a place to offer your wishes and prayers, become pregnant with ideas and energies and let creativity bubble up. Her Red Rocks speak of enhancing the feminine qualities of inspiration, creativity, flow and inner beauty and how to ground that ancient Earth wisdom through the sacral and root with red flames of fire. Her biggest message is that we are all connected, each of us a thread woven into the ether. The feeling of nothingness and everything is important at this time. You hold a place in something beautiful, a meaningful place. Don't doubt your brilliance, your gifts and what you offer this world.

Song of the Nightingale

ELEMEMT:
Air △

MEANING:
Tending to the broken

You see the nightingale singing through the tree tops, as golden light spills from her beak. Her songs are full of uplifting energy. Birdsong connects us to the angels, as birds are the messengers of the angelic planes – their tones are true and pure and go straight to the heart to help it to open. Perhaps the angels are trying to get your attention, to show they are supporting you. Notice the little things, the feathers and numbers around you as they show themselves to you to reassure you that you are not alone in this.

The Nightingale sings so loudly and boldly for such a shy, timid little bird. If you drew this card, the Nightingale knows when matters of the heart are on the line for you, and helps you to find the inner confidence to make some noise, encouraging you to speak up for what feels right.

Valuing the infinite wisdom locked in your being, the Nightingale is an extremely secretive bird that will guide and protect mysteries and tender spaces inside you. It wishes to soothe the spirit and sing to the soul to awaken. Watch as its tiny form flies through the back of your heart. It is just a little thing, waving its light to your deepest hidden chambers to bring forward wisdom with its song. It can guide you out of any darkness.

The Nightingale's medicine is one of bravery. It calls forward your deepest desires and supports you in finding ways to voice and express them creatively.

Sphalerite

ELEMEMT:
Earth ▽

MEANING:
Ancient energy channels reconnecting

The Sphalerite on this card wished to be painted in the centre of a giant cosmic web that shimmers different colours, highlighting the vast interconnectivity of everything and everyone to you. It reminds you that as much as you matter to the whole, you are also a small piece of it that works symbiotically with all. It reminds you of the importance of patience and perspective at this time.

Sphalerite is a connector of ancient energy streams, above and below the Earth. She attracts to you what you need in this moment to support your healing journey, whether it is elven energies or galactic frequency coding. Through Sphalerite, you can connect with the teachers and scribes of your past, asking them to show you the ancient streams of consciousness you have worked with, as she will re-open those streams to run through you once more.

A mystic, grandmother energy, Sphalerite is grounded and balanced in her approach. She is a teacher stone. Lean into her and offer her your worries and she will give you a higher perspective. She is a wonderful stone for guidance when embarking on a spiritual journey. Sphalerite speaks:

"My energy has the ability to weave high streams of information, vibration, sound and light into the body, where they will be woven in with the very deepest parts of your being to your core, to bring feeling and light to the dark spaces.

See my energy form as a grounding web of light that surrounds you from above – a net that will gather up all scattered energy and merge them back into your body, mind and soul.

There is nothing more grounding than love, as we connect in with the love Mother Earth has to offer, together we support in magnetizing all elements within the inner kingdoms back to you. All of your elemental

fragments, eleven light codes and faery light will be
magnetized back to you in an elemental reclaiming.

Hold me in your hands and in your heart,
as I activate in connection with your heart's intent,
and call back energy like a magnet."

Stellar Beam Calcite

ELEMEMT:
Fire △

MEANING:
Acceptance; uplifting;
interdimensional travel

Stellar Beam Calcite is a rare type of calcite that will help in manifestation and reaching higher planes. On the card, it points upward, directing you toward these planes, and it speaks of acceptance and asks you to accept who you are and not fight internally with yourself because you are perfect. Its energy is so high-vibrational that it speaks from the universal heart and mind. Stellar Beam Calcite is very philosophical, wise, reassuring and kind, bringing a surge of uplifting joy and positivity, ready to raise you up and encourage you. It aligns the emotions in the solar plexus and heart in this understanding and this spiritual law of acceptance.

This law of acceptance is one of the first spiritual laws: this is the conscious choice to drop all resistance. It isn't about approval or liking something, it's about letting go and allowing your life to flow and unfold without getting in your own way. After you have worked with Stellar Beam, you are energized and attuned with its vibration and are ready to go deeper with it. The stone will ask you the questions you may have been avoiding: about yourself, who you are and where you are going. It will not ask you these questions to test you, merely to highlight to you the things you are observing, offering a new perspective on a situation or a relationship.

Stellar Beam Calcite speaks:

"Don't reject the parts of you that you feel are negative, whether it's a part of your personality, character or a physical aspect. You are a multifaceted being, you have many angles, layers, dimensions and aspects, and all are perfect. Learn to embrace those parts of you that you might not think highly of. Shine light on them and welcome them as part of you and you find wholeness in the beauty of all of you.

Yes, you are perfect, you are a reflection of the Earth and stars, which are perfect and in divine order.

You might feel you have flaws, but to somebody else, these are not flaws at all, they are strengths.

You are stronger than you know."

Sun Jaguar and Rainbow Obsidian

ELEMEMT:
Earth ▽

MEANING:
Meet your needs first

The Jaguar walks between worlds, attached but unattached, of the world but not in the world. If you drew this card, she asks: how can you walk this world and not attach to everything? This is her biggest lesson. You are in a world that says that you "need" many things to be happy, when all you really need is unconditional love and freedom to express yourself. At the Jaguar's core is motherly love and tenderness, but she knows her wild, fierce and free nature and steps into it with ease and grace. She knows who she is and imbues this energy on you now. Know who you are, sift through the stories, projections and false narratives you play in your mind, or that you have taken on from others or inherited from your ancestors. Make time to get to know yourself and what you want and need

– your needs should come first at this moment.

Rainbow Obsidian is a powerful healer. It comes to support your emotions with gentler energy than Black Obsidian. When you walk with the Jaguar, you are expanding in rainbow light. Rainbow Obsidian comes to ground this spiritual light into your aura and physical body, working in harmony with your energy field, supporting an integration of this light. Rainbow Obsidian will help you get to the root of the emotional trauma and distress that have been holding you back, helping you cut ties with that past.

Its energy surrounds you now like a blanket, dissolving unloving thoughts. It is a voice of reason, bringing clarity and focus to your innate powers, wishing you to look deeper into how you show up and love yourself, boosting your self-esteem and self-worth. This is an invitation to look to what you feel is holding you back at this time. What is this tether teaching you about yourself? If you let it go, what would happen?

Tiger Lily and Pyrite

ELEMEMT:
Fire △

MEANING:
Dancing around the edges;
accepting yourself

Tiger Lily reminds you of the dance of the ego, wanting to fit into something that does not serve you. At times we can all feel like outsiders, that we don't fit in and struggle with being accepted. You may be questioning where you belong in society, and all the social structure around you. People like you are extremely important, and as much as they can feel uncomfortable, individuals and groups on the outskirts or the fringes of society are needed. You are the changemakers, the ones wanting a new vision of life, a new lifestyle and a new sense of community. It takes courage to be brave and own who you are and what you feel and believe. But the more you do this, the more you will illuminate the path and lead by example for yourself and others, and Tiger Lily will help you along the way.

Tiger Lily is proud and colourful. It stands tall, high from the ground and upright. It is sure of who it is and radiates its jewel-like tones for all to see. It exists as a masterpiece in its surroundings, dancing and singing in such a free way. Tiger Lily called crystals to dance with and settled on Pyrite as this holds a bold fire energy to ground in everything we want and need. Pyrite also helps us to ground emotions through the lower chakras to bring stability and build stronger new foundations. This is the energy you need at this time – the playfulness to remember you are free and do not have to fit the mould. Lean into the fires of passion and creativity to build this new foundation you are working on, which is one of change and divine love and acceptance.

Vanadinite

ELEMEMT:
Fire △

MEANING:
Muse; creative rivers are flowing

Vanadinite is a lead mineral that forms in beautiful bright red hexagonal prisms, ranging from bright red to orange-red shades. This stone wanted to be painted growing from the ground, in an otherworldly "fiery" desert scene with the deer, which symbolizes the youthful energies of innocence and trust. Vanadinite represents beauty, fresh potential and new life. She is associated with the qualities of innocence, youth, self-confidence, intelligence and independence, and encourages you to express yourself, and to explore and discover. Tune into the energy of the three Graces around her. These Graces are the three daughters of Zeus and Hera: Aglaia (Brightness), Euphrosyne (Joyfulness) and Thalia (Bloom). She offers the beautiful images of young women dancing and singing in a circle, communicating that she is very much connected to goddess energy.

Vanadinite is here to tell you that you are about to experience an abundantly creative time, and her medicine comes to really stir something beautiful within you, a soulful creative expression. She will help boost and stir those fires of creativity within your lower chakras so you can express what is in your heart. Whether it's through colour and art, writing and movement, she tells me that her role is the "muse". She inspires, but *only* inspires (she is very clear on that) and you must nurture and birth the ideas yourself. Have her close when writing, as she is known to aid writers' block, making her a perfect companion for creative writing.

Let her fire energy of motivation guide you by boosting your own energy levels. Through the mental field she connects strongly to the third eye chakra to help you focus with clarity on your aims and goals, creating the powerful action to carry you forward in confidence and ease. She will help you stick to your goals and ignore any distractions.

Vivianite

ELEMEMT:
Earth ▽

MEANING:
Revealing your heart's truth

Vivianite wished to be painted in the landscape of the Amazon rainforest where it is from, with vivid green nature energies and an orange amazonian butterfly symbolizing freedom and flight. Vivianite holds the keys of the emerald ray of healing and truth, offering them to you at this time to shake you up, to bring the purest form of truth forward through you.

Its direct voice helps you get to the "truth of the matter", and in all situations it whispers that it is the root of truth. This card asks you to look at your current situations and discern the energies around you. Take some time to work out which energies, people, places and situations best deserve your energy at this time. As it works closely with the mind and mental field, Vivianite will help you to clearly see the course of action and conviction in the pathway to take. Once you have dived into its messages, visualize it sealing your aura with a brilliant emerald-green light, and bring all of your energy back into your heart and body with your breath.

It has a gentle side too, which you can work with once you show it your trust. Its energy of love and peace is here to help anyone who has experienced emotional and physical trauma as a child. It allows you to come to terms with it, bringing you to a compassionate, heart-centred place. It creates a wave of serenity and peace to wash through you and help bring closure.

Watermelon Tourmaline

ELEMEMT:
Earth ▽

MEANING:
Get out of your head

Watermelon Tourmaline is an extremely rare mineral with a red to pink centre due to its manganese content, and a green outer rim that is caused by inclusion of iron. As you can see on the card, when sliced it looks like a watermelon, hence its name. Watermelon Tourmaline's energy is one of elevation. Its light is high frequency and fast, opening your crown chakra to connect you with the universal mind, which is completely balanced. The universal mind is filled with high vibrations we can travel with, as we realize that everything is connected from the trees to the animals; we are all connected in one mind, one heart. Sometimes we need a reminder to get out of our heads and into our hearts, or to provide a balanced bridge between the two. Watermelon Tourmaline connects us to the cosmic heart and higher mind through our higher chakras, for elevated perspective on situations. Its energy will shake up your mental field and help you let go and dissolve limiting beliefs.

The energy of this card is one of creation, aligning you to the infinite cosmic void where stars are born and life is created. Ask Watermelon Tourmaline to help you create that light bridge through heart and mind: both need to be aligned for you to be able to look, plan and reach ahead. Now is a time to tend to your mental wellbeing, get out of your head and into your heart and create with abundance.

Wounded Warrior

ELEMEMT:
Air △

MEANING:
Masculine healing; father line

The sword is an important focus on this card, to show strength, will and power. It is painted in front of Mount Kailash in Tibet, which is symbolic as it is the focus of the masculine ray on this Earth. This card brings attention to the divine masculine energy within and around you, and asks the men to soften and receive. You are being asked to lay down your sword, honouring the warrior within you and your strong, courageous heart. This will be hard for some, as the fight is long gone, the battles are over and all that's left are wounds of times gone by. Yet this battle is not with others, it is with yourself. Do not hold onto the burdens of the past, but bring together what feels torn apart. You will always be a warrior of love, but you can lay down your sword and experience the weightlessness of freedom.

Serve yourself above all else

There is a great shift at this point in Earth's ascension cycle, a changing of the guards, and as your energy releases from a site, a new protector's energy will over-light it. The watchers, the protectors and the caretakers of the land are being asked to reconnect with those parts of them that are still serving. They are still protecting on ancient timelines, and your role is fulfilled. You can release your energy from those sites and sacred spaces, pilgrim routes and temples.

Woodpecker Spirit

ELEMEMT:
Earth, Air ▽ △

MEANING:
Don't give up; time is all you need

The Woodpecker Spirit wanted to be painted happily and conscientiously pecking away at a branch high up in the trees. He sings of the importance of surrendering to divine timing, which is the universal truth that everything happens at the perfect moment. He asks you to remember that not everything is within your control. This could present itself as a challenging obstacle in the path, a meaningful coincidence or simply a gut feeling.

The Woodpecker Spirit is one of the most intelligent spirits in the animal kingdom: he is smart, perseveres with determination and is proud of his strength. His energy moves fast and sharp, as he taps away obstacles in his path, and he doesn't give up. If you are connecting with the Woodpecker Spirit through this card, you have a deep affinity with the heartbeat of the Earth and her rhythms and cycles. It is time to create more ceremonies in your life through rituals in nature. Create with intent: things are happening behind the scenes, and there is much going on under the surface for you.

Tune into your body's rhythm and natural flow and honour it. Are you listening to your body? If you are moving through an active time of creativity and ideas, push forward with them, and persevere and believe in yourself. Make sure you move without any interference from other people's projections of beliefs. Give yourself rest time, but also know that soon great opportunities will arise and light for you to expand into will come.

Acknowledgements from the Author

Thank you to Nikki, for bringing this deck to life, for capturing the essence of the stones and their energies so magically.

Thank you to my Watkins family for all the love, support and time they have poured into this deck and the supporting book *The Songs of the Stones*.

Huge gratitude to the Ancestors and energies of the crystalline and plant kingdoms for weaving their wisdom through this deck,

And lastly, but most importantly, thank YOU for reading this, for investing your time, for journeying with me, trusting, surrendering and allowing. I am so grateful for you.

Acknowledgements from the Illustrator

A big thank you to Katie-Jane for entrusting me once again to bring her vision to life through the artwork for this deck, our third collaboration!

Thank you to Watkins for their support and guidance in creating this oracle deck and helping us bring it to the world.

Much love to my ever supportive inner circle – my family, friends, partner and dog.

About the Author

Katie-Jane Wright is a spiritual author, crystal whisperer and guardian, ceremonialist, healer and teacher based in the UK. Her healing lineage was active from a young age, when she began seeing and working with spirits of many dimensions, her healing hands passed down through her mother line. She is keen to help others remember the ways we used to work with the stones in the past, and the multi-dimensional ways we can work with them now. She offers transformational crystal workshops, events and healing retreats around the world, with a focus on crystals and sound.

She created her brand &Crystals in 2016, aiming to teach people how to connect with energies through their heart. Through her store she sells small collections of rare minerals and crystals skulls, all handpicked and sourced from collectors that are guided to her. The integrity of the stones and connection with the land and people they came from is of the utmost importance to her. She works with small family mines in Brazil in an ethical and sustainable way. This wish for respect and integrity can be found woven through the crystal book that is a companion to this oracle deck: *The Song of the Stones*, where she has journeyed with the land and guardians of the stones to tell their stories. Her healing crystals collections have been sold in Anthropology stores worldwide. Katie-Jane has written another crystal book called *Crystals: A Conscious Guide*, as well as oracle decks *Spirit Animal Wisdom* and *Earth Alchemy*, with illustrations by Nikki Strange.

About the Illustrator

Nikki Strange is an illustrator and designer who works from her studio based in North London. She runs her own label Nikki Strange Ltd which specializes in hand illustrated paper goods and accessories with a touch of magic. Through her brand she endeavours to create beautiful products with meaning and purpose that help individuals connect better to themselves and the world around them. In her work she uses watercolours and inks to create her imaginative designs, working with them digitally to create layered and intricate compositions that hope to transport the reader or buyer. Nikki's work has been sold and seen in the likes of ASOS, Fenwicks, Topshop, Selfridges and Urban Outfitters.

WATKINS
1893

The story of Watkins began in 1893, when scholar of esotericism John Watkins founded our bookshop, inspired by the lament of his friend and teacher Madame Blavatsky that there was nowhere in London to buy books on mysticism, occultism or metaphysics. That moment marked the birth of Watkins, soon to become the publisher of many of the leading lights of spiritual literature, including Carl Jung, Rudolf Steiner, Alice Bailey and Chögyam Trungpa.

Today, the passion at Watkins Publishing for vigorous questioning is still resolute. Our stimulating and groundbreaking list ranges from ancient traditions and complementary medicine to the latest ideas about personal development, holistic wellbeing and consciousness exploration. We remain at the cutting edge, committed to publishing books that change lives.

DISCOVER MORE AT:
www.watkinspublishing.com

Read our blog

Watch and listen to
our authors in action

Sign up to
our mailing list

We celebrate conscious, passionate, wise and happy living.
Be part of that community by visiting

 /watkinspublishing   @watkinswisdom
 /watkinsbooks   @watkinswisdom